DISCARD

The Little Butterfly

A Random House PICTUREBACK®

The Little Butterfly

by Sherry Shahan

For Elizabeth Spurr
from your nectar-sipping friend

Random House 🏠 New York

Text and photographs copyright © 1998 by Sherry Shahan. All rights reserved under International and Pan-American
Copyright Conventions. Published in the United States by Random House, Inc., New York,
and simultaneously in Canada by Random House of Canada Limited, Toronto.
http://www.randomhouse.com/
Library of Congress Cataloging-in-Publication Data
Shahan, Sherry. The little butterfly / by Sherry Shahan. p. cm. — (Random house pictureback)
SUMMARY: Follows a newly hatched caterpillar from birth to metamorphosis, mating, and migration.
ISBN 0-679-88809-8 (pbk.)
1. Butterflies—Life cycles—Juvenile literature. [1. Butterflies.] I. Title.
QL544.2.S465 1998 595.78'9—dc21 97-28745
Printed in the United States of America 10 9 8 7 6 5 4 3 2 1

The winter sun shines on a field of wildflowers in California. Hidden from view, a tiny egg glistens on the leaf of a milkweed plant. The dark egg splits open and a monarch caterpillar crawls out.

The little caterpillar is very hungry. She eats her eggshell. Next she chooses a crunchy milkweed leaf. The leaf is quickly riddled with chew marks. Soon the whole leaf disappears.

The little caterpillar is still hungry.

She has eight pairs of legs. They help her cling to the milkweed plant. Her front legs grasp the food while she eats. *Crunch, crunch, crunch.*

Monarch caterpillars only eat milkweed. Still, she has a decision to make. Should she munch on another leaf? Or chew on a plump pod?

The little caterpillar chooses a pod. She eats and eats. Then she eats some more. Leaves and pods disappear. Thick milky sap drips from the chewed plant.

Milkweed is poisonous to larger animals, including people. But milkweed doesn't harm the little caterpillar. Instead, it makes *her* poisonous to eat. Birds have learned that eating these boldly striped caterpillars will make them sick.

Other insects join the feast. Rosy red aphids and black-and-red beetles slurp up the sap. Ladybugs fly in to feed on the aphids.

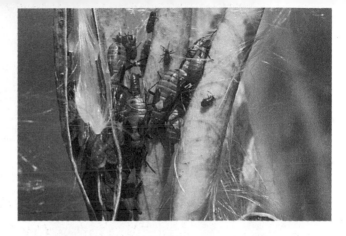

A spider spins a web to trap a buggy meal: flies and beetles. Sometimes a spider will even try to catch a caterpillar. But our little caterpillar crawls safely onto a higher stalk.

The little caterpillar is getting bigger and bigger. Soon she will be too big for her own skin! The caterpillar's skin doesn't stretch. To keep growing, she must shed her old skin. This process is called "molting."

When she is ready, her old skin splits open and she wiggles out. The caterpillar is already wearing her shiny new skin underneath.

With a new set of stripes, she goes back to her favorite activity —eating milkweed. In a single day she eats two times her weight in food. She is storing fat for a time when she won't be able to eat.

The little caterpillar eats and eats. She grows and grows. Then she molts again. She sheds her skin four or five times during this part of her life.

It has been two weeks since the caterpillar crawled out of her egg. Suddenly her body begins to stiffen. Is she ready to molt again? Not this time.

Slowly, the caterpillar crawls up the trunk of a tree. Out on a branch she spits up a mat of stick silk fibers. She sticks like glue to the silk mat and hangs upside down.

The little caterpillar is ready to shed her skin one last time. But this time she doesn't get a new set of stripes. Instead, she forms a mummy-like sack called a "chrysalis," or "pupa." This hard sack protects her from harm.

The chrysalis hangs from the branch like a bright green jewel. During the next nine to fifteen days, amazing changes take place inside. The little caterpillar is changing into a butterfly. This remarkable process is called "metamorphosis."

Now the chrysalis is as thin as paper. Take a closer look. Can you see the black-and-orange wings of the creature inside?

Finally the sack splits open and a butterfly pops out. The newly hatched butterfly can't yet fly because her wings aren't strong enough to lift her body. She clings to the sack and waits for fluid to flow from her body to her wet wings. They open and dry in the warm sun.

The striking colors of the wings, just like the caterpillar's bold stripes, warn birds that the little butterfly is poisonous. Some other types of butterflies have similar orange and black wings. This fools predators into thinking that they are poisonous, too.

Soon the little butterfly flies high into the branches of a eucalyptus tree in search of food. After all, she hasn't eaten in two weeks! But she isn't hungry for milkweed anymore.

Instead, the butterfly drops onto one of the tree's flowers. She unrolls her long tongue and uses it like a straw to sip the sweet nectar. From now on, her whole diet will be made up of nectar and water.

Thousands of monarch butterflies make the eucalyptus grove their winter home. At dusk they gather in the tops of the trees. Each butterfly hangs upside down with its wings over the butterfly underneath it. They look almost like shingles on a roof.

On warm days the eucalyptus grove is alive with mating butterflies. The male butterfly gives off a perfume-like scent to attract a female. He struts in front of her, opening and closing his wings. After mating, the butterflies begin a long journey north.

Every year thousands of monarch butterflies make a journey called "migration." In northern regions, the chilly fall air tells them it's time to fly south to warmer weather. Some monarch butterflies travel up to two thousand miles to reach their winter homes. Later in spring, the butterflies begin to head back north. But no one butterfly lives long enough to make the entire round-trip journey.

The female butterflies lay their eggs along the way. Their children will continue the journey from wherever they are.

Our little butterfly lays her eggs under the leaves of milkweed plants. The underside of a milkweed leaf shields the eggs from rain, sunshine, and predators.

Three or four days later, a hungry caterpillar eats its way out of the egg casing. The little caterpillar munches a bunch of milkweed. It is still hungry, so it eats some more.

Crunch, crunch, crunch.

The caterpillar munches a whole milkweed leaf.

Soon it is too big for its skin.

Do you know what happens next?